WRITTEN BY GLORIA FOWLER + ILLUSTRATED BY MIN HEO

PARIS IS A BEAUTIFUL CITY IN FRANCE;
PLEASE COME VISIT,
SHOULD YOU HAVE THE CHANCE.

THE FRENCH CALL IT *PAREE*,
AND THERE IS SO MUCH TO SEE;

COME WITH ME AND YOU'LL SEE,
IT'S A GREAT PLACE TO BE!

BONJOUR IN THE MORNING,
S'IL VOUS PLAÎT IF YOU PLEASE;

MERCI TO GIVE THANKS,
AND JE T'AIME TO *PAREE*!

FIRST STOP, THE BOULANGERIE FOR OUR BREAKFAST CROISSANT,

THEN LATER ON IN THE DAY, THE PÂTISSERIE, FOR WHATEVER YOU WANT!

LET'S YOU AND I RIDE A BOAT DOWN THE SEINE,

UNDER THE BRIDGES,
FROM BEGINNING TO END.

NEXT STOP, THE ARC DE TRIOMPHE,
WE'LL CLIMB HUNDREDS OF STAIRS;

WE'LL WIND ALL THE WAY UP,
'TIL WE'RE OUTSIDE IN PLEIN AIR.

LET'S RIDE THE MÉTRO,
GET LOST, AND HAVE FUN;

ACROSS THE WHOLE CITY,
THE SUBWAY DOES RUN.

THEN ON TO THE LUXEMBOURG GARDENS WE'LL GO,
WE CAN SAIL LITTLE BOATS;

THEY ARE PAINTED BRIGHT COLORS,
MADE OF WOOD, AND THEY FLOAT.

AT NIGHT WE'LL DRESS UP AND SEE THE BALLET,

UNDER THE DOME OF THE PALAIS GARNIER.

WE'LL VISIT THE ISLAND THEY CALL ÎSLE DE LA CÍTE,

PRETTY STAINED GLASS WINDOWS?
SAINTE-CHAPELLE—RIGHT THIS WAY.

THEN NEXT THE CATHEDRAL
THEY CALL NOTRE DAME;

AND AFTERWARDS ICE CREAM,
THE BEST: BERTHILLON.

LATER ON WE'LL GO SHOPPING
ALL OVER THE CITY,

SUNGLASSES, SHOES,
ALL OF IT PRETTY.

LET'S TAKE A TRAIN
TO VERSAILLES FOR THE DAY;

WE CAN ROW OUR OWN BOAT
ON THE LAKE FAR AWAY.

IN THE AFTERNOON FOR A REST,
WE'LL SIT IN A CAFÉ:

SIPPING HOT CHOCOLAT
AND ENJOYING THE DAY.

OR MAYBE INSTEAD,
MACARONS AND SOME TEA?

HOW FUN WOULD THAT BE,
JUST YOU AND ME?

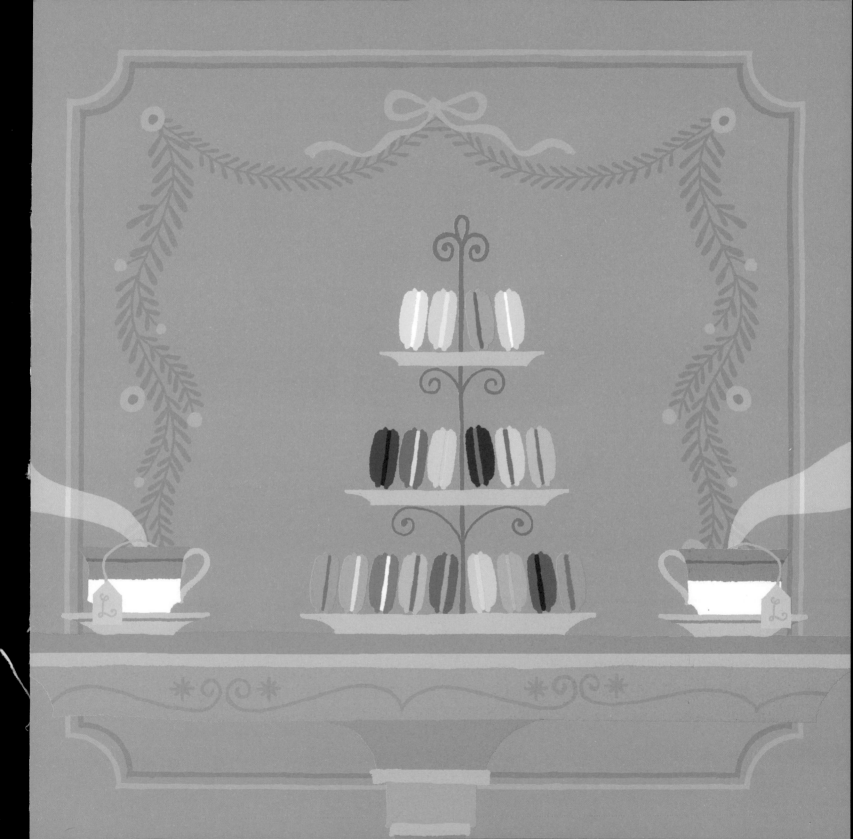

LET'S SIT AND WATCH
ALL THE FASHIONABLE PEOPLE STROLL BY:

DID YOU SEE ALL THE PUPPIES IN PURSES, OH MY!

WE'LL VISIT THE MOST FAMOUS MUSEUM OF ALL;

THE MONA LISA IS HERE,
THE LOUVRE IT IS CALLED.

ALONG THE SEINE,
WHERE THE BRIDGES DO CROSS;

FROM PONT NEUF,
MAKE A WISH,
WITH A COIN WE CAN TOSS.

GETTING SLEEPY?
A PICNIC LET'S TAKE;

A NAP IN THE SUN,
PARIS PLAGE, 'TIL YOU WAKE.

AND HERE'S AN OLD TRAIN STATION,
NOW THE MUSÉE D'ORSAY,

FROM DEGAS TO MONET,
SUCH AN AMAZING ARRAY.

LET'S RIDE A CAROUSEL,
AROOOUUUND WE GO!

UNTIL IT'S TIME FOR A CRÊPE,
I CANNOT SAY NO.

NEXT, SHAKESPEARE AND COMPANY,
FILLED WITH GREAT BOOKS;

LET'S SIT ON A BENCH AND HAVE A GOOD LOOK.

LET'S CLIMB SACRÉ-COEUR,
TO THE TOP,
FOR THE VIEW;

SUCH A BEAUTIFUL CHURCH,
ON A HILL,
ON THIS RUE.

LATER ON,
LET'S TAKE A TAXI TO THE CHAMPS ÉLYSÉES:

FANCY SHOPS AND CAFÉS,
WISH WE COULD STAY.

AND OF COURSE, THE EIFFEL TOWER
ALL THE WAY UP TO THE TOP;

YOU CAN SEE THE WHOLE CITY,
AND THE LIGHTS NEVER STOP.

LET'S TAKE PICTURES
OF ALL THESE GREAT SIGHTS,

FOR MEMORIES AND DREAMS,
DEEP IN THE NIGHT.

AT THE END OF OUR TRIP,
AU REVOIR AND BONNE NUIT!

JE T'AIME MY DEAR ONE,
AND JE T'AIME TO *PAREE*!

FAMOUS SIGHTS FEATURED IN THIS BOOK:

EIFFEL TOWER [EYE-FUHL]:   THIS FAMOUS TOWER WAS BUILT IN 1889 FOR THE WORLD'S FAIR.

SEINE [SEHN]:   THIS IS THE RIVER THAT FLOWS THROUGH PARIS.

ARC DE TRIOMPHE [ARK DUH TREE-ONF]:   THIS FAMOUS MONUMENT COMMEMORATES THE FRENCH REVOLUTION.

MÉTRO [MEH-TRO]:   THIS IS THE SUBWAY SYSTEM ACROSS THE CITY.

LUXEMBOURG GARDENS: THIS IS A BEAUTIFUL PUBLIC PARK AND GARDENS.

PALAIS GARNIER [PAH-LAY GAHR-NYAY]:   THIS IS THE OPERA HOUSE THAT IS ALSO HOME TO THE PARIS BALLET.

ÎSLE DE LA CÍTE [EEL DUH LAH SEE-TEE]:   THIS IS ONE OF TWO ISLANDS IN THE SEINE.

SAINTE-CHAPELLE [SAHNT SHA-PELL]:   THIS GOTHIC CHAPEL WAS BUILT IN 1239.

NOTRE DAME [NO-TRUH-DEM]:   THIS FAMOUS GOTHIC CATHEDRAL WAS BUILT IN 1163.

BERTHILLON [BAIR-TEE-YOHN]:   THIS IS A WELL-KNOWN ICE CREAM MAKER.

VERSAILLES [VAIR-SY-UH]:   THIS IS A FAMOUS ROYAL CHATEAU WHERE LOUIS XIV LIVED.

LOUVRE [LOO-VRUH]:   THIS IS ONE OF THE WORLD'S LARGEST AND MOST FAMOUS MUSEUMS.

MONA LISA: THIS IS A FAMOUS PAINTING BY LEONARDO DA VINCI FROM THE EARLY 1500s.

PARIS PLAGE [PAH-REE PLAHJ]:   THIS IS THE PARIS BEACH THAT IS CREATED ALONG THE SEINE EVERY SUMMER.

PONT NEUF [PAHN NUHF]:   THIS IS A FAMOUS BRIDGE AND IS ONE OF 37 BRIDGES OVER THE SEINE.

MUSÉE D'ORSAY [MYOO-ZAY DOR-SAY]:   THIS MUSEUM USED TO BE A TRAIN STATION AND WAS BUILT IN 1898-1900.

DEGAS [DUH-GAH]:   HE IS A FAMOUS FRENCH ARTIST WHO LIKED TO PAINT BALLET DANCERS.

MONET [MOE-NAY]:   HE IS A FAMOUS FRENCH IMPRESSIONIST WHO LIKED TO PAINT LANDSCAPES.

SHAKESPEARE AND CO: THIS IS A WELL-LOVED BOOKSTORE ON THE LEFT BANK.

SACRÉ COEUR [SAH-KRAY KUHR]:   THIS CHURCH IN MONTMARTRE IS THE HIGHEST POINT IN THE CITY.

CHAMPS ÉLYSÉES [SHAH ZAY-LEE-ZAY]:   THIS IS ONE OF THE MOST FAMOUS STREETS IN THE WORLD.

GLOSSARY:

BONJOUR [BON-ZHUR]:	GOOD DAY
S'IL VOUS PLAÎT [SEEL-VOO-PLEH]:	IF YOU PLEASE
MERCI [MEHR-SEE]:	THANKS
JE T'AIME [ZHEH-TEM]:	I LOVE YOU
BOULANGERIE [BOO-LAH-ZHREE]:	BAKERY
PÂTISSERIE [PAH-TEES-REE]:	BAKERY THAT SPECIALIZES IN DESSERTS
HOT CHOCOLAT [SHO-KOH-LAH]:	HOT CHOCOLATE
MACARON [MAH-KAH-RON]:	SWEET, ROUND, AND COLORFUL DESSERT
CRÊPE [KREYP]:	A THIN, LIGHT PANCAKE
PLEIN AIR [PLAN-ER]:	PAINTING IN OUTDOOR DAYLIGHT
RUE [RU]:	STREET
AU REVOIR [OH REH-VWAHR]:	GOODBYE
BONNE NUIT [BUH-NWEE]:	GOODNIGHT

WRITTEN BY GLORIA FOWLER
ILLUSTRATED BY MIN HEO

ART DIRECTION + DESIGN: GLORIA FOWLER
COPY EDITING: SARA DEGONIA
PRODUCTION: MEGAN SHOEMAKER

SPECIAL THANKS:
CATHY WAGNER
STEVE, MILES, AND LOLA CRIST

FOR MORE CHILDREN'S BOOKS AND PRODUCTS VISIT US AT:
WWW. AMMOBOOKS.COM